How to Understand
Your Parents
and Maybe Like the Ones
You Love

HOW TO Understand Your Parents

and MAYBE LIKE the ONES you LOVE!

by Robert Baden
Illustrated by Will Hardin

CONCORDIA®

Publishing House
St. Louis

To Mom and Dad,
who understood me better
than I understood them.

Copyright © 1987 Concordia Publishing House
3558 S. Jefferson Avenue, St. Louis, MO 63118-3968
Manufactured in the United States of America

Library of Congress Cataloging-in-Publication Data

Baden, Robert, 1936-
    How to understand your parents and maybe like the ones you love.

    1. Youth—Religious life. 2. Family—Religious life. I. Title.
BV4531.2.B227 1987   248.8'3   86-31695
ISBN 0-570-04467-7 (pbk.)

1 2 3 4 5 6 7 8 9 10 DP 96 95 94 93 92 91 90 89 88 87

CONTENTS

1 Why Parents Say the Things They Do   7

2 "Your Appearance Will Ruin
My Reputation"   12

3 "Your Friends Are Fouling Up
My Guidance"   20

4 "With Those Grades,
You'll Be a Failure"   28

5 "Pick a Career Now, or You'll Get Lost
in the Rat Race"   36

6 "Learn to Save;
I Can't Support You Forever"   43

7 "What You're Doing Can Hurt Us Both"   51

8 "Don't Mention That Word
In This House!"   60

9 "What Do You Mean,
You Don't Like Church?" 66

10 Maybe Parents *Are* People
After All 74

WHY PARENTS SAY
THE THINGS
THEY DO

Can any teenager understand his or her parents? I think
so—although some of my friends aren't so sure. Indeed, trying
to convince some teens that they can understand their parents
seems a little like trying to convince Daniel that he could *talk* the
lions out of eating him. They probably wouldn't have listened—
but, at just the right moment, God stepped in and caused that
adventure to come out all right. I have the courage to suggest
that your relationship with your parents can improve, because I
believe—no, I know—that God will step in here also and bless
your efforts.

God created man and woman with the potential to be parents, and He commanded them to use that potential. Sin, however, turned what God had planned to be a happy, cooperative,
perfect relationship into one that often has lots of problems. It
didn't take long for those problems to appear. Adam and Eve's
first son murdered his brother. Eli the priest and King David had
problems with their sons. Even the 12-year-old Jesus realized
His parents didn't fully understand Him.

But God didn't quit trying to improve family relationships
in biblical times, and He hasn't quit trying now. He tells children

to honor and obey their parents, and parents not to make their children angry. Because He knows both will fail to keep these laws, He provides forgiveness for both parents and children. This enables them to forgive each other. He sent His own Son, Jesus Christ, to die on the cross to make and seal the bargain. He stands by with an overflowing cup of blessings to pour on those who hear His Word and seek to follow His will. Since I know all this is true, I'm not afraid to share some ideas that might make your life with your parents a bit better. I pray that you will find them useful.

Looking Ahead

Did you notice the title of this book? I assume the topic interests you somewhat, even if you get along with your parents most of the time and communicate fairly well with them. You probably have times when you just can't figure out your parents, times when you have trouble even liking them. It is those times that we want to concentrate on in this book.

But I don't intend to give you a sermon on how you're supposed to behave in order to please your parents. I assume you are a Christian, as I am, but I certainly won't use that fact as an excuse to lay a guilt trip on you. You already know what's right and wrong. Rather, as the title says, I want to help you understand your parents by sharing some of the reasons parents are the way they are. I want to help you understand why they feel certain ways about things—such as the way you dress, eat, or talk, or the friends you choose, and why they're so concerned about how you do in school, about the career plans you are making, the way you spend money, how you drive the car, and your attitudes about church, God, and morality. When you understand where—and why—parents stand on these subjects, you might feel more comfortable talking about them with your parents—and thereby grow in understanding. Such sharing, unfortunately, is usually hard to do, both for you and for them. Even when you and your parents share the same Christian faith and love each other deeply, it's still hard to do. But faith and the trust that God loves and forgives us when we fail can make it possible for sinful parents and sinful children to love, to forgive, and to understand each other anyway.

The Problem of Differences

Understanding and communication may seem impossible when the people involved are significantly different from one another. Parents look and act different from the way you look and act. Their clothes, their hair, their choice of television shows and movies, when they go to bed or get up, the things they eat (some parents even like brussels sprouts and broccoli), the music they listen to, their goals and attitudes—they're often different, aren't they?

I won't argue that differences don't exist; of course parents are different. But would you really want them to be just like you? Can you imagine your mom in a punk haircut or your dad wearing the latest style of tight, shiny pants? Put your trendy words and language into their mouths. How does it sound? Is this what you want from your parents—actions and ideas identical to yours? I don't think you want parents who are just like you or look or act as you do. I believe you'd just like a little respect, understanding, and appreciation. You'd like your parents to accept you the way you are, the way you think.

Interestingly enough, most parents seek about the same thing from their children—a little respect and acceptance for what they think and are. Of course, they also expect—and have a right to—obedience, but even that comes a lot easier when respect and acceptance of differences are mutual. But neither respect nor acceptance will take place without understanding. While the stated goal of this book is to help you understand your parents, the secondary goal surely is to help parents understand you. And they might—if you're willing to talk and listen to each other and to put yourselves in each other's shoes for a while.

Two Secrets About Parents

Although parents and teens are different from one another, the difference need not be an insurmountable obstacle to their understanding one another. Think for a moment about the question "What is an adult?" Answers such as "old-fashioned," "workaholic," "old and out-of-it," "always too busy to talk to me," "interested in things that don't interest me" may come to mind. All of these things may be true sometimes. But here's another way to see adults, a secret that may be helpful in understanding them: "grown-up teenagers."

You know how life is as a teenager. You know how it feels to be hassled by parents, teachers, employers, and even friends. You know how hard you work to make friends, to be accepted, to gain respect and attention. You know about problems with the opposite sex and the difficulty of getting a job. You know about frustrations with how you look and feel. *Most of these feelings still plague adults.* Parents also feel pressure from employers, spouses, friends, and even from their own parents, your grandparents. Parents struggle to move ahead in their professions, to earn attention and respect. They, too, sometimes have problems with the opposite sex. Some may be struggling to get a job or to change jobs. And, while acne and voice change may not be a problem for adults, overweight, hair-thinning, and overall health are objects of concern. The only difference between teens and parents is that parents have been plagued by these feelings/problems for a few more years.

This secret shouldn't depress you about growing up. Rather, it should help you understand your parents by showing that they aren't as different from you as you may think. If you can accept this similarity and use it as a communication aid instead of a barrier, you may start to overcome another adult tendency that hinders good, healthy conversation—the tendency to view you as children, even as infants. And that's where the second secret comes in.

When parents say things like "Don't act like a baby," or "Grow up," they aren't trying to insult you. Rather, they are showing their own difficulty with letting you be grown-up. I don't expect you to like that notion, but try to understand why parents might have it. They remember very well the time when you really were a baby. They remember a helpless, crying little person who needed all their attention, all their protection, all their guidance all the time. They got used to taking care of everything for you—from feeding you to changing your diapers. Now add to that the fact that, in their minds, the time between then and now has been short. As a result, parents can't quite believe that their teens have grown up and don't need attention, protection, and guidance all the time. You can feed and dress yourself now, and they sometimes forget that. And when they do realize it, they often regret it, because if you are now 14 or 16 years older, so are they. That's tough on parents and something they'd like to ignore.

These, then, are two secrets that you need to know and understand about parents if you're really going to try to walk in their shoes and do your share in building a bridge of communication.

Take the Lead in Understanding

Perhaps you're saying it isn't fair to put so much burden on you. Well, maybe not; but parents in general haven't done a very good job of taking the initiative in communication. They've found it far easier to make rules, to inflict punishment, to yell a lot, and to wash their hands of the younger generation. If there's any hope at all, I think it has to come from you. I'm sure that if you know a little more about parents and what makes them tick than you did before, you might be able to build the bridges that they haven't. Of course, if you've given up on your parents, if you've decided you don't love them, then you have a problem that no book will solve. The title of this book assumes your love, no matter how buried it is. I believe that most of you do love your parents, just as they love you, even when no one verbalizes it. It's liking and understanding them that are the real problems. Fortunately, those problems can be overcome.

So that's where I'm coming from. I'm praying that I will be successful in sharing some ideas with you, and I'm asking you also to pray that things between you and your parents will be the way God intended them to be and that you'll have the courage to do your part—and more—to help make it happen. God is ready to bless your efforts and your home. His Word is filled with help. Rest assured that God is eager to help you and bless you as you undertake this task.

As we go along, I'll try to be as honest with you as I can be, both in what I feel and think as a parent, and in what I felt and thought in the 1950s when I was your age. I know that was a long time ago, but maybe we'll find out that some things weren't really all that different.

"YOUR APPEARANCE WILL RUIN MY REPUTATION"

It is almost impossible for a teenager to spend five minutes in a room before an adult finds at least several aspects of his or her appearance or behavior with which to be dissatisfied.

All of you, no doubt, can recite the typical criticisms:

"Your hair is too long."

"Your shirt is out."

"Your jeans are too tight."

"Your shoestrings are untied."

"Don't wipe your nose on your sleeve."

"You need a shower."

"Don't crack your knuckles."

"Don't talk while you're eating."

"Don't belch."

"Don't bite your fingernails."

Such a list could continue forever. It literally goes from head (and the hair on top of it) to toe (and the shoe that covers it). It omits almost nothing between the two—not the cosmetics, clothing, or general appearance, not the smells, sounds, or actions.

Please—don't defend yourself just yet. Remember the book's title: *How to Understand Parents.* Pleasing them might come a lot later.

Why Parents Are So Concerned

Just why do parents react so strongly to your appearance? What makes their "standards meter" go off the board so regularly, so predictably? Since I am a parent and have reacted myself to what I have seen on and heard from my four children, I think I know. I'm not sure I like to admit it, but I said I'd be honest.

Society considers children—including teenagers—a direct representation of their parents. Society reasons that children are an obvious product of parental input. The Bible also suggests such a connection. Here are two examples: "Train a child in the way he should go, and when he is old he will not turn from it," Prov. 22:6; 1 Sam. 2:12–36 tells the story of how the sons of Eli disgraced their father. Parents clearly get blamed or praised for the actions and appearance of their children. Naturally, parents prefer praise.

You know how easily you get embarrassed? Parents are no different—and in their eyes, their children sometimes cause the most embarrassing moments. Yet they desperately want to look good in the eyes of others—their friends and society as a whole.

They want others to look at their children and say nice things, such as "My, your children are well-behaved," or "Your children are always so clean and neatly dressed." But when their preschoolers have a fit in the grocery store, or their teenagers tear up the road, parents "know" what others think of them—because they've thought the same things about other parents. Why can't my kids be *model* children? they think. Of course, perfect children don't exist in this world. So such an attitude on the part of adults is grossly unfair—but it's real. And you have to understand this reality as part of understanding where parents are coming from. You don't have to like it or agree with it; just understand—and maybe, then, empathize a little with your parents.

Remember how you felt when your little sister wet her pants as you were playing with your friends? Remember how mortified **13** you were when your little brother asked you what happened to your other boyfriend/girlfriend as you and your current date walked out the door? Remember how you giggled in embarrassment and maybe wanted to die when your date burped loudly as you were eating with your family in a restaurant? Even if such things haven't happened to you, I'm sure you dread the possibility.

Similarly, parents fear that their children will do or say something to embarrass them—and that fear keeps them worried. As a result, parents react to and make seemingly unnecessary rules about their children's appearance.

I remember my reaction when suddenly, in the middle of a church service, I noticed that one of my sons (who was neatly dressed in his sure-to-please-others Sunday suit) wasn't wearing any shoes. None. Just his socks. I was furious and mortified. In an angry whisper, I asked him why. He said that he couldn't find his church shoes and I was outside in the car honking for him to hurry. When I asked him why he hadn't said anything, he said he didn't want me to get mad. I thought about condemning him for not showing proper respect in God's house, but down deep I knew I was more concerned about my reputation than I was about God's. I knew my son could worship without shoes. I knew he wouldn't catch a cold. I knew that shoes and clothing make no difference to God. But I was utterly terrified at what others would say or, more likely, think. "What terrible parents not to supervise their child's appearance in God's house! Don't they have any control over their children?" Or "Poor child; his parents are so poor that they can't afford shoes for him."

All reason goes out the window when such things occur. To minimize such occurrences, parents make rules and pass pronouncements, usually just after the embarrassing event. "If any one of you ever goes to church again like that, . . . " The threat that finishes the sentence varies according to the culture from which we come.

How Children React to Parents' Concerns

Teenagers particularly react negatively to these rules and threats. Their sinful nature takes over and prevents cooperation.

They tend to react by testing the rules and resorting to literal actions. The teenager who hears "You will not wear blue jeans to school" comes down the stairs the next morning dressed in shorts or a jogging suit, responding to the parental outburst with "But you said I couldn't wear *blue jeans*"—and the issue soon becomes a struggle of opposing wills. Parents hope that new rules and stricter punishments will result in appropriate behavior; teenagers hope that, if they challenge the rules long enough, their parents finally will give in or give up.

Teenagers react in another way, too. After several such experiences, teenagers generally conclude that, since their parents are concerned for their own image, they (the teens) possess a great power "to keep their parents in line." Teens learn how to embarrass their parents—or at least threaten to—in order to get their way. "I won't get my hair cut unless you get me the new cassette tape I've been wanting." "I'll wear that dress to church if I can have the party at our house next weekend." This "embarrassment technique" is not unique to parent-teen relations; it has caused divorces, revolutions, even global war. No one pretends that its use will solve anything or make life better in the long run, but teenagers do it anyway—partly because, from a human point of view, the normal growing-up process requires young people to establish separate personalities. But in a Christian home, sinful confrontation/conflict can shake the faith of the family.

Embarrassment is not the only reason parents pick on appearance. Many parents, genuinely concerned about their teenagers' health, criticize them for not taking care of their body, complexion, or teeth. Parents also worry legitimately about the *teen's* reputation (even more than theirs) when he or she dresses or looks like a member of some musical group that has questionable morals. Nor do they want the teens to appear ridiculous to teachers, employers, or others whose judgments can affect the teen's future. Granted, an adult's definition of "ridiculous" may well differ from yours, but parents are concerned about appearance and will do almost anything to enforce standards they believe are in accord with conventional expectations of the adult world.

Understanding this problem does not solve it, but understanding is essential before any solving can take place.

Opening Doors
for Communication

Solutions begin with understanding and continue with communication. But it's not easy to talk when a conversation goes like this:

Father: "You are not going to wear those clothes outside this house."

Daughter: "Why not? Give me one good reason why I can't!"

Father: "Because I said so!"

Daughter: "That's no reason!"

Father: "It's reason enough as long as you're living in this house!"

Such a conversation is not communication. Communication requires a sender and a receiver; here only sending takes place. Neither father nor daughter is hearing the true communication behind the words of the other—so no one seeks a solution. Parental force will probably win this particular battle, but the war has only begun. This daughter will now turn on her heel with some comment about parents, retreat to her room, slam her door, and begin planning for the next attack. No solution; just a stalemate. Worse, repetition of this kind of "conversation" can culminate in genuine dislike on both sides.

Solutions won't be easy. Teenagers want involvement in decisions, and parents want to make the decisions "for your own good." Neither party eagerly compromises because each believes his or her side is right and the other wrong. Parents say, "But we are responsible for the welfare of our kids"; and teenagers say, "But we have a right to make our own decisions." To a degree, both are right and both are wrong. But until they talk, until they realize that sin is controlling their relationship, until they ask for and offer forgiveness, no solution will be forthcoming. Nothing will improve until they begin to live out the words of Eph. 6:1–4, "Children, obey your parents in the Lord, for this is right. . . . Fathers, do not exasperate your children. . . ."

But how does one begin the process of communication? "They're always too busy" is the teenager's excuse for not trying; "Kids are in a different world" is the parents'. And right here, I believe the secret to success lies with the teenager. Yes, it means that you take the first step—probably the first several. But I think that parents often fear initiating a true conversation more than you do. They are afraid you'll reject their overtures—and sometimes they hope you will, because they really aren't sure how to do anything except make rules and pass judgments. Parents come from a generation where even less talking with parents occurred than does now. Life was simpler. Children were less independent, and certain subjects just weren't talked about. For this reason, many parents really don't know how to talk about things; it's easier to give orders because that's what most of them learned from their parents.

Most parents really would like to be able to talk to their children about serious subjects, but they simply are afraid and don't know where to start. That's where you come in. You have often talked about serious subjects in school or at church, and you have much more experience talking to other people than most parents do—on the telephone, face to face, in small groups, with members of the opposite sex. Initiating true communication with your parents won't be easy for you, but considering it in this light may make it easier. In any case, it probably will be easier for you than for your parents.

Carrying on a Conversation

When you do initiate a conversation, your parents will know you really want to talk. They'll suspect you want something—and even if you do, you need to start by acknowledging that you need help with something. Admit that it's hard for both of you to talk, that you understand about embarrassment *and* their concern for your reputation and health. Express your wish not to hurt them by what you do, admit your own shortcomings and failings in the past, and ask for their forgiveness. If you do, most parents will immediately admit that they haven't been perfect either. Help them recognize that you understand—that's the key word—where they're coming from. Or, if you don't understand, ask them how it was with such matters when they were your age. And, above all—even when it's hard to say the words the first few times—tell them that you love them, and assure them that you forgive their shortcomings. Then, be willing to com-

17

promise on what you want, even if you don't say it at the outset. And, if your parents want to know why you want to dress or look a certain way, tell them—but don't rely on that old teenage copout, "Because everyone else does."

Why can this work when confrontation fails? For at least two reasons. First, because you aren't challenging their authority as parents, but actually seeking their advice and approval and second, because parents aren't out to make you look bad in the eyes of others, in spite of what you may think sometimes. Sure, they want you to avoid extremes, but they don't want you to wear what they wore 25 years ago any more than they want you to look like the newest, most outlandish rock group. They want you to be clean, neat, and relatively modern; but mostly they want you to look and act "appropriate for the occasion." Parents define appropriate in terms of their own standards, I'm afraid, but open communication can adjust that definition in time. Basically, appropriate means (to many parents) wearing something less extreme to church than to a party, with school clothing being somewhere between the two. Occasions when you're with relatives and/or adults may be closer to church than a party, but final decisions can come from talking it out—calmly.

The more you talk, the more you'll find out about each other. Your parents will laugh as they show you their high school or college yearbooks and see what they wore "such a few short years ago." Your parents may seem "out of it" now, but a little conversation may reveal just how "with it" they were in their generation—and how eager they are for you to be popular and successful in yours.

Moving On
Toward Joyful Relationships

Will I guarantee success if you do these things? Of course not. Your parents, you, I—we are sinners and cannot create a perfect world. But God expects us to work toward more perfect relationships with each other. He has given your parents to you to love and to honor, and He has given you to your parents to love and to lead. He expects parents to be models, not monsters; but He knows all of us will act like monsters far too often. Therefore, He offers us His free forgiveness through Jesus, expecting us to offer it just as freely to those around us, especially those in our family. Open conversation, saturated with Christian love, won't guarantee perfection, but it will lead toward a home life that is a joy for God to see and a pleasure for us to live.

3

"YOUR FRIENDS
ARE FOULING UP
MY GUIDANCE"

I'm fairly certain that you and your parents agree about the importance of friends. Like you, your parents value their friends. They enjoy spending time with them. Your parents respect their friends, listen to them, worry about their problems, and miss them when they move away.

Why, then, does the mention of your friends so often turn into a problem—an attack on you as too dumb to pick the "right" friends or too weak to be as good as your "well-behaved/smart" friends?

Perhaps I'm jumping the gun. Maybe your parents never hassle you about your friends and, in fact, like them all. If so, you are indeed fortunate. More likely, though, you do hear comments that reflect negatively on your choice of some of your friends, how much time you spend together, and what you do. When that happens, you probably get irritated. You know that you have picked friends worthy of your time and respect and that you spend your time together completely above board.

When Parents Are Concerned About Your Friends

As I mentioned in chapter 1, being a parent means being protective. Many parents want to save their children from mistakes, from learning the hard way, as they did. They look back to their own teen years and still feel the pain of being hurt or betrayed by false friends. Your parents may still feel the guilt of giving into temptation in order to be included in a group and/or to maintain status. So, in part, your parents are really saying, "I love you enough to want to spare you a life—or a moment—of pain and guilt," even though you are willing to take the chance.

They also may be responding, the only way they know how, to admonitions from God to parents such as "Bring them up in the training and instruction of the Lord" (Eph. 6:4). Your parents may be trying to help you have only those friends who will influence your life in a positive, Christian way.

So even when their words say, "You ought to pick better friends," try to understand the possible message of loving concern actually behind the words.

How You Can Respond

Whatever words your parents choose in saying something less than glowing about your friends, you're likely to perceive them as an attack upon you. And, like most people under attack, you're likely to become defensive or offensive.

A defensive person might retreat without saying anything, using the parents' comment as another bit of evidence to prove how ignorant and unfair parents are. This person might spend less and less time at home and more time with the friend, especially if the friend's parents seem more open-minded and accepting than his or her own.

A person on the offensive—who might also be an offensive person—usually returns the attack, even hoping to outdo the attacker. "You can't possibly know anything about friends since you never had any"; or "I can see why you don't have any friends"; or "What about your friends Weird Wally and Nasty Nellie?" Cutting comments like these might sound clever and

21

feel good at the moment, but they dig ditches in a relationship rather than build bridges. They might even result in reprisals.

On the positive side, open communication about friends between you and your parents will strengthen your relationship and increase your parents' confidence and trust in you. It only takes a few easy steps.

First, if your parents ask a direct question such as, "Do your friends smoke?" or "Do you think you should be seen with someone who dresses like that?" try to accept the question in the spirit of loving concern in which it probably was asked (even if it didn't sound very loving). If you can, express appreciation for their concern.

Second, answer the question. You have nothing to hide. Show that you trust your parents and respect their concern. (Sometimes we parents need to know that from our teenagers.)

Third, ask your parents to tell you about the friends they had when they were teenagers—how and why they were chosen, what they did together, why certain friendships broke up, what they did or said when their friends did something wrong, etc. Or, if that topic's already been exhausted, get your folks to talk about their present friendships. Parents, like most regular people, like to talk about themselves. You'll find it interesting, and you'll find they're usually more willing to listen to others (that's you) with an open mind. A word of caution: If your parents trust you enough to open themselves up to you, don't share the information with others or use it against them later. That isn't fair.

Fourth, help your parents understand why you chose the friends you did—especially if your parents can't see what you saw in this or that person who's "so different from you." Here again, try to understand where your parents are coming from. They see fine young people at church, from school, in the neighborhood. Inevitably, parents assume that you will choose friends who seem most like you—in appearance, age, actions, even income level or race. That often happens. But you also encounter other people—at school, work, church, in sports or music or other activities—to whom you're drawn because of some less obvious similarity. Perhaps you sing in the same choir section, are lab partners, tried out for the same sport or school play, or simply have lockers next to each other. To you, the similarity seems obvious. But, since your parents don't know that, they see only the differences (which they might not like), question your judgment, and suggest a change.

When that happens, calmly point out the similarities you see and enjoy, and, without betraying any confidences, point out the differences in that person with which you disagree and which won't change you for the worse. For example, even though you may be friends with the person using the locker next to you, you may be repelled by that person's sloppiness. When you point out to your parents that you're still keeping your bedroom neat in spite of the "bad influence," they'll worry less about your choice of that friend at least.

Helping Your Parents Get to Know Your Friends

When tension fills your house, you may be tempted to use peer friendships—and even friendships with your friends' parents—as a substitute for friendship with your parents. You can see that happening when teenagers give their parents the cold shoulder, storm out of the house, and use their friends' shoulders to cry on. Being replaced by an outsider threatens parents and sometimes tempts them to work harder on breaking up that other friendship. (I'm sad to have to admit that parents sometimes do such things.) That's why your parents need to know that your friends are no threat to them. Take the initiative and create opportunities for your parents to meet and get to know your friends firsthand. In so doing, you will quickly break down their parental worries.

We parents do tend to jump to conclusions, to put the worst construction on everything. I remember when one of our sons became part of a group that played a popular simulation game on a regular basis, going from home to home to do so. The first time they came to our house, my wife and I were mortified— and very suspicious. We saw only the motorcycles they arrived on and the long hair they had. Our fantasies blossomed. Finally, we asked our son whether this group's agenda included drinking or drugs, fearing the worst. "Hardly," he laughed. "When I first joined the group, they clearly explained to me that they wouldn't tolerate any drinking, smoking, or drugs." Two of that group **23** now teach school, one studies law, another medicine, and one is an editor in a publishing company. I probably chose a rare example, but it illustrates the way parents may imagine the worst until they learn to know your friends.

So have your friends come to your home so that your parents can meet them and see them in action. You don't have to worry about parents wanting to be part of that action; they just want to feel secure with what they see. Of course, if you're embarrassed about your parents—as many teens are—you'll have to deal with that. After all, your friends might end up liking your parents. If your friends are the kind to be proud of, you'll all survive the ordeal—and you will have done your part to improve the relationship between your parents and you.

When Parents' Concerns Are Justified

What if some of your friends are, at least partly, involved in things that wouldn't meet the approval of your parents? Are you willing to consider the possibility that you might be better off not associating with them? If you can answer yes to that, you truly are verging on maturity—more than some adults who don't possess the willingness or ability to evaluate their acquaintances honestly.

I realize that Christian young people don't go out looking for friends who live immoral or inappropriate lives. But people's true personalities are not always obvious at first. It's after the friendship has begun that concerns may arise. You may begin to feel pressure to do things just because the group does. You may be invited or even encouraged to smoke, drink, use hard drugs, or do and say other things contrary to God's law and your Christian conscience. Even having Christian friends doesn't guarantee freedom from problems and difficult temptations.

Just being with certain groups or a certain person can raise flags of suspicion in your parents. For example, if your friends smoke and you don't, your breath, hair, and clothing will still have the characteristic odor when you walk in the front door. If you have developed an open line of communication with your parents, you will be able to convince them that you are not participating in the unacceptable activities. Even better, you'll be able to talk with your parents about—and get help with—handling the pressures you feel and the conflict between friendships and personal principles.

However, the pressures and temptations will continue to plague you. The time probably will come when you will have to decide if these friends and their tempting activities are worth your time and energy. Supportive parents at that time will be, literally, a godsend.

When Parents Are Too Impressed by Your Friends

If your friends maintain the same Christian standards that you try to, you are indeed fortunate. Treasure friends like that; they are blessings from God Himself. They'll even help build your parents' confidence in your wisdom, judgment, and maturity.

But friends like that also bring an ironic consequence. Your parents may say, "I wish you'd do such and such the way your friend does." How frustrating to have your friend's moments of best behavior pitted against the overall impact of your full-time personality in the home!

Or your parents may say, "I just met Vicki Virtuous and Randy Righteous today. They're such fine young people. Why don't you ever spend time with them? They'd make such nice friends."

Now, you know Vicki and Randy very well—certainly better than your parents do. You know that Vicki and Randy have mastered the art of image-making. You know that they can con adults with a perfect image and, at other times when no adults are around, be real pains, doing and saying things that would curl your parents' hair.

The suggestions made earlier can apply to this situation, too. Once again, force yourself to hear your parents' love and concern behind words that may seem more like a condemnation of you. They probably aren't. Parents use strange sentences to communicate private dreams, such as "I pray that everyone will respect you throughout your life," or "I pray you won't be boxed into a corner all your life like I am, without the freedom to make the choices you have now." Parents don't usually say things like that directly; such words reveal too much about a parent's feeling of failure, either on the job or in marriage. Parents know the pain of poor choices and want to spare their teens from having it, too. Your parents may even want to spare you pain that might come from knowing about *their* pain. That's a lot of love. Just knowing that concern can help you understand the message behind words that seem to be criticizing you.

Also, keep in mind that your parents can't know Vicki Virtuous or Randy Righteous as well as you do. They have only seen the surface. Although your parents may not be willing to believe the true story, keep in mind that they are more concerned that you have good friends in general than Randy and Vicki in particular.

Admittedly, suffering under a comparison to Vicki or Randy gets a lot harder when these two people are perfect—all the time, it seems. Then it really gets tough explaining why Vicki and Randy aren't your friends.

How You Can Respond

Once again, try not to be defensive or offensive. Refusing to say anything or saying something like "Oh, Mother! You don't know anything!" cuts off communication and only confirms parental suspicion that you don't want anything to do with "good" friends.

Rather, be willing to talk about it calmly and try to turn the conversation to your parents and their friends when they were teens. Talk about what they did, not with a "see-you-weren't-perfect-either" tone, but as a means to help them understand your choice of friends. More than likely, your parents and their friends weren't Miss Virtuous or Mr. Righteous all the time either—though they may not want to reveal too much about that. That's one reason parents get uncomfortable; they see you doing some of the same questionable things that they did. Is that hypocritical? Perhaps—but often conversation will help you and your parents understand each other's fears and hopes, even if all the details aren't shared.

Then explain how you do pick your friends—common interests, similar abilities, the need for acceptance, the ability to have fun together. Your interests may be totally different from Vicki's and Randy's. What they may think is fun may bore you. And it's impossible to have anything but less-than-perfect friends. We all—including Vicki and Randy—"have sinned and fall short of the glory of God" (Rom. 3:23). For true friendship to exist, friends need to be forgiving of each other, as well as supportive in the struggle to live a Christlike life. Your parents undoubtedly know these things but your calm reminder will let them know that you take your friendships seriously and with Christian maturity.

And one final thought: If your parents frequently comment negatively on the subject of friends, even after you've tried the things mentioned, they just may not know you very well. If not, some serious talking needs to be done—not just about specific friends, but some honest sharing of feelings and ideas, hopes, dreams, and prayers. When you keep the lines of communication open—even if change isn't immediate—you'll find your parents eventually relaxing, growing more trusting, and being able to enjoy both you and your friends a lot more.

You may even arrive at a new problem: your best friend's mom may use you and your relationship with your parents as a model for their family. You probably never thought of yourself as Miss Virtuous or Mr. Righteous. Wouldn't that be interesting!

4

"WITH THOSE GRADES, YOU'LL BE A FAILURE"

Perhaps the last thing you want to think about is school, and especially parental questions about it—grades, homework, teachers, after-school activities, behavior in school, what you wear, and so on and so on. Well, you're not wrong if you think parents are concerned about your education and schools and teachers, and your attitude toward and relation with them. You've probably heard most of these comments somewhere along the road:

"Finish your homework before you watch any television."

"You've got to study at least two hours every night—and I mean every night!"

"You call these grades? These are disasters!"

"What do you mean you lost another textbook?"

"I'm sure Miss Fidditch is really a very nice person."

"I don't care if you'll never use history or grammar; they're good for you!"

After a shouting match with your parents about school, you may have concluded that they don't understand at all about your life or needs or interests. Perhaps you resent working all day at school just as they have at the office or in the home—but you have to study until bedtime while they watch their favorite television shows. It doesn't seem fair; and you may be wondering when you get a chance for a little relaxation—and whether school is even worth it.

Parents Were Students Once, Too

As a teacher, I affirm that school *is* worth all the problems, but I won't lay that on you until we talk a bit about parents and why they feel and act the way they do about school and studying. First of all, most of the same things they say to you they heard from their parents 20 or 25 years ago. Believe it or not, not all parents loved everything about school, willingly did their homework, or brought home straight A's on every report card. No way! When they were your age, they probably felt and did much the same as you do.

Parents, however, don't want you to know they weren't perfect students and didn't learn everything they were supposed to. Maybe that's why they may become uncomfortable when a former schoolmate comes for a visit. Maybe that's why they hope you aren't listening when the friend says to your dad, "Remember the time you put that cat in the refrigerator in the teachers' lounge?" Or to your mom, "Remember how we all got caught smoking by Mr. So-and-So in 10th grade?"

Before we start to find ways to communicate with your parents on this subject, it's important for you to know that most parents were very much like most of you are—maybe even worse. Most of them copied a paper from someone else, peeked at someone else's paper during a test, passed notes during a boring class, smoked illegally in the rest room, skipped school or played sick at home, called teachers unflattering nicknames, hated history or grammar or math, brought home a bad report card or a failed test, had to stay after school, and argued with their parents about things at least once during their junior or senior high school years. If you don't believe it, ask them. Get them talking about how it was when they went to school. Who knows? Once you get them going, they may not stop.

Parents Know the Value of Education

Just because you had or have some problems with school should not cause you to conclude that school serves no purpose in your preparation for life. Actually, I suspect you know that. Your parents, though, may not be able to explain to your satisfaction why a subject is valuable or necessary for life. Even teachers have trouble doing that. But they know that they understand the world, the people in it, and the way it works *now* because of some of those classes they thought weren't practical or worthwhile way back then. They know it, and they want you to get all the benefits that you can from a good education. So they push hard, probably too hard at times, to get you to do "what's good for you."

If you attend a private or a Christian junior or senior high school, you have an added piece of evidence that they care. Most of these schools cost money, lots of it—money that could be spent otherwise if you were going to a public school. But these parents believe Christian education is worth the expense. They want their children to have an education based on Christian morals. If you attend such a school, you need to understand and to appreciate the sacrifice your parents are making, even if you don't always like the school you are attending.

Unfortunately, parents will sometimes use this "money matter" as a club. "We're spending $2,000 a year to send you to that school, and you'd just better make it worthwhile." And they see to it that you do. Each time you goof off on a test, you're likely to be reminded that you're wasting money—hard-earned parental money—when you aren't perfect. You feel extra pressure on every aspect of your education—attendance, grades, study, activities, attitudes, etc.—so much, sometimes, that you may resent ever having been sent to a Christian school. Parents shouldn't use that approach; but if they do, try to accept it as evidence that they really want you to have the best and not blow the chance you have.

30

Parents also have seen that an education—high school, college, even graduate school—not only prepares you for certain professions, it also helps you advance in any employment. Even hourly workers who have some college education have the advantage over those who don't. And parents with little education, as well as those with graduate degrees, push teenagers to get all the education they can because "we want you to have what we didn't," or because "we expect you to get at least as much as we did." Even though your parents might have been imperfect students themselves, they now know that the more you understand about God's world and His people, the more you will enjoy it in all its fullness.

That's at least some of where parents come from on this subject—and the reason why they are so intent on making sure you take advantage of the educational opportunity you have. Solutions to conflicts on this subject can come if you work to build understanding in at least three areas:

1. Understand that parents were probably much like you with regard to school. Show interest in their educational background and get them to talk about it.

2. Understand that parents reflect and reinforce the pressures of society toward education. Accept this given, and you may avoid many purposeless arguments.

3. Find ways to communicate your needs and priorities so that you can work in time for things other than homework, things that also are important in a young person's life—friends, sports, music, even television and other leisure activities.

Realizing that Education Has Changed

However you and your parents communicate, whether by getting them to talk about their school experiences or by talking about problems you're having with certain classes or teachers, you and your parents will discover that education is very different from what it was 25 years ago. I don't mean that it was easier or harder then; each generation believes it had the hardest time in school.

Rather, you are learning different things than your parents did. If your parents are 35 or 40 years old, they grew up as the space program began, during the initial impact of the civil rights movement, when the presidents were Eisenhower, Kennedy, and Johnson. You probably consider their literature and music to be old-fashioned or call them "golden oldies." Such things are not better or worse, just different.

As a result of such differences then, if you're looking for help with a certain class and if they're eager to give it, you may find they are unable to do all you'd like. The mathematics you are learning is different and far more advanced than most parents received, even in college—and unless we specialized in that field, you may already know more than we ever did. If we did study it, we may have forgotten it from lack of use. The same may be true in psychology or sociology in which, as the joke goes, "the questions stay the same but the answers change." Ways of studying history or the English language have changed, as have techniques for learning foreign languages. Perhaps science, though, presents the widest gap. Unless parents work in professions using scientific knowledge on a daily basis, they will be almost ignorant about anything scientific from the last 20 years, the time during which science and technology have advanced a great deal.

Fortunately, many parents are learning a little about using computers, though they don't understand why this "miracle" works. Most teenagers take computers for granted and wonder how parents can be so "dumb." Let's face it, even television still causes me to pause in awe every so often as I wonder how those pictures get through that little wire.

Realizing that You Can Help Each Other

This is not to say that your parents learned nothing of value; they received the best education possible at the time. But the differences between your learning and theirs can cause frustration, envy, and even resentment if they are not understood and accepted by both sides. Seeing my children use a computer almost embarrasses me (even while it makes me proud); kids aren't supposed to know more than parents. As a result, I could have created a chasm between us. Fortunately for me, my kids helped build a bridge between us. What little I know about a computer comes from my teenage son; he has taken the time to show me how to do certain things (most take several showings before I understand), and he patiently calmed my fears that I'd ruin something by my ignorance. I deeply admire his ability and appreciate his patience. I have enjoyed our communication on this subject, and I find him a good teacher—a better teacher, I fear, than I am a student. Of course, before that communication could take place, I had to accept and admit the fact that I didn't know everything, and he had to learn how to share what he knew without looking down on me or losing respect for me as a parent. I'll never beat him at any of the computer games—but, then again, he still needs help with a few "old-fashioned" things.

Some parents don't realize that they can't answer all your questions in math or English, and they may resent it when you call a friend for the help they'd like to be able to give. Too many parents have sat for hours trying to remember how to do binomials when their teenager's five-minute call to a friend could have solved the problem. Teenagers need to be real diplomats to help their parents come to this realization.

Parents can, though, offer valuable suggestions for book reports, "tricks of the trade" on writing a research paper, tips on studying for a test, or inside information on the "ancient history" of the Korean or Viet Nam wars. And, most of all, parents have valuable ears on which to try out an idea, eyes to read through the rough draft of an essay, minds to ask "what-do-you-think" kinds of questions, and hearts with suggestions on how to get along better with certain teachers. Parents have been there, and often you only need to ask to get the benefits of their experience.

At the same time, encourage your parents to read and discuss with you the novel you are studying in literature. You can explain to them the intricacies of higher math. You can use your science experiments as a stepping stone to discuss the ethical questions now raging through the scientific community.

In general, you and your parents can share with each other education and learning as you know it from school *and* life. With this kind of cooperation, family education truly can become a two-way street, with both contributing richly to the process. **33**

Realizing that Life
Is More than School

Even though most parents realize that life is more than school and school work, they may get almost paranoid if you aren't doing homework every minute you're home. They fear that if you do poorly in school, you will lose a chance at college or a good job. (Unfortunately, some parents use homework to keep kids off the streets at night and confined to their rooms while the parents watch television or entertain guests. When that's true, the parents have a serious problem.)

You and your parents need to talk about priorities and to create a realistic schedule that does not make you a slave to study. Remember, it was somebody's *parent* who long ago wrote the saying, "All work and no play makes Jack a dull boy." That person understood well that education comes in many more forms than a classroom.

Discuss your family's schedule and rules. For example, while the rule "no television before homework" generally may prove helpful, it also means you have to miss the early evening programs oriented toward youth and family. Mutual conversation may lead to a reasonable arrangement that allows some television before study time—if you can show that you can get your homework done in time for a good night's sleep. Mutual communication will provide also for those rare nights when you actually have no assignments, and you won't hear the suspicious comment, "Don't you have any homework to do?" Mutual communication will also help parents understand that television sometimes can be an important form of education—though your parents probably will insist that any program endangering your homework must have some "educational value."

Regarding going out on school nights—can you compromise? Parents usually will agree to evening athletic contests or play rehearsals on school nights (if you get your homework done before such activities begin). But no matter what you say or do, they probably will oppose movies, dating, late hours, etc. on school nights. While you may sometimes resent having to do school work while your parents read or watch television, try to avoid angry comments like "You never have to do anything at night." Such comments are sure to cause continued conflicts. Besides, watch your parents' lives closely, and you'll see it's generally not true. Most parents use the evening to work on house projects, prepare for or attend church or civic meetings, do the family finances, plan/arrange family events, etc. Rather than verbally attacking your parents, you're far wiser if you accept school responsibilities. Share with your parents some things about school—your classes, your books, your questions, your joys and frustrations. They have gone through school and, if gently reminded, will realize what you're going through—and will take the time to show interest, to give support, and to understand you. That's the kind of family life that God envisions for us and the kind He has promised to bless abundantly.

"PICK A CAREER NOW, OR YOU'LL GET LOST IN THE RAT RACE"

"What are you going to be when you grow up?" Your parents, relatives, and other adults probably have asked you this question since your earliest days. Maybe it hasn't always been in the form of a question; maybe they said, "John is going to be a doctor/engineer/pastor/teacher/scientist when he grows up." Or "Mary is going to be a nurse/lawyer/radiologist/teacher when she grows up."

Perhaps the first time you heard these "predictions," you were pleased, both by your parents' image of you and by their confidence in your ability to reach these goals. But now, as time for college and career decision-making grows closer, you might not feel quite so pleased. Perhaps you fear the additional years of education these prestige positions require; perhaps you doubt whether you have the ability to achieve these goals. Perhaps parental confidence has eroded a bit through the years into occasional comments like "You'll never amount to anything," or "Can't you ever do anything right?" Dreams that parents have when their child is a toddler often dwindle into nightmares coming from what they perceive as their teenager's laziness or total lack of ambition.

Few teenagers and their parents escape an almost unavoidable encounter over career plans and choices. However, a little understanding about parents on this subject can help you better handle both the encounters and your own feelings about your career options.

Parents Are Career Conscious

If their teenager hasn't made a career choice yet, the parents tend to attribute the indecision to ignorance or unconcern. As in other conflicts, they tend to base their feelings on where they are after 15 or 20 years of career experience rather than on where they were when they were 14 or 16 or 18 years old. They wonder why you aren't as concerned about such matters as they are now, and they tend to talk about "facing the realities of the real world out there." When they see you laughing and listening to contemporary music or lost in the intricacies of a computer or video game, they conclude that you want only to have fun and enjoy life—while they worry about paying for your food, clothing, shelter, and transportation.

While parents may not understand your situation fully, they do understand the situation in the world of employment. Perhaps they have experienced the reality of job consolidation and layoffs. They may have had to retrain to keep a job. They may have experienced the difficulty of moving up in a company or of changing jobs in an economy struggling with interest rates and foreign competition, stretched by overpopulation and streamlined by modern technology. Parents have *legitimate* concerns for their own careers and *understandable* fears about yours—fears which increase when they think that you are going through life in blissful ignorance of the realities they know so well.

Although your parents may not agree with me, I believe that most adults take sole credit for their own achievements rather than acknowledging that getting into college and into certain careers was easier back when they got started. Technology had not yet eliminated the need for many jobs, and they, the postwar "baby boomers," had only begun to enter the job market. I remember well my greatest concern when I graduated from our denomination's teachers college: *where* would I be placed to teach, not if. At the time, I felt some resentment that the officials in the church had the power to put me where they wanted, but no gratitude that the placement service had made my job search an easy one. Graduates today feel just the opposite; they are not sure a place will be available and are generally grateful for all the assistance given them by the placement service.

Whether or not parents understand or accept this reason for the difference between then and now, they correctly perceive the difficulty of young people getting started in a career today. They have seen the frustration of young people just out of college who are denied jobs because they lack experience and who lack experience because they can't get a job. Parents know that this "Catch 22" situation exists. That's one reason why they are so insistent that you do well in school and set your career plans early.

Sometimes Parents Push Too Hard

Parents often don't understand that the way teenagers are won't change just because employment is getting tighter. They forget sometimes that they were equally undecided and unconcerned when they were your age. Back then, other things—popularity, a car, a good time, the opposite sex, identity—were far more important to them just as they probably are to you now. "The future will take care of itself when I get there" characterized their philosophy of life—as it does each generation when it is young. And, once established as adults, each generation forgets—and wonders what the younger generation is coming to and why it is so unconcerned about its future. We adults have the tendency to forget the way we were and to become "experts" on the way others ought to be.

Another parental concern arises over the career you choose. Parents want their children to succeed in a career that they and society respect. Parents generally want their children to do one of two things: (1) If parents are successful and happy in their own careers, they tend to want their children to "follow in their footsteps," to take over the business, to become a doctor or teacher like they are, to be a "chip off the old block"; or (2) they want their children to be more than they are, to become what they didn't or didn't have the chance to be. These parents want their children to have all they didn't have, partly so that their children will be happier and partly so that the parents can live through their children the life they (the parents) were denied.

Both of these parental desires cause problems for teenagers. Few parents honestly say to their teenagers, "Be the best you can be at whatever you want to be." From the time of their children's birth, parents consciously or subconsciously begin to program little Debbie or little David into the doctor or astronaut or politician or computer whiz who will save the world and gain wealth and glory. If you think about this a bit, that desire for you is understandable. Your parents want the best for you. They want you to find joy for yourself and bring credit to them, and they want to feel that they helped you along the way to your success. For the infant or child, this causes few problems. Most young children readily accept and repeat their parents' desires for them: "I'm going to be a pastor like my dad"; "I'm going to be the first woman president of the United States"; "I'm going to be a banker and make lots of money"; "I'm going to go to Africa and tell everyone about Jesus."

The problems begin when youngsters become young adults. Suddenly the courtroom, the seminary, the White House, First National Bank, and Africa seem a lot closer—and the emotional cost of additional study, work, expenses, and stress becomes more real. How can you say to a parent (who still has the same old dream for you) that you really want an entirely different career? How many parents will respond to the end of their dream with a hug and a handshake and the words "Then be a good one"? If the dream ends abruptly for the parents, an argument—often a very angry one—may occur.

Some Special Career Concerns

Career choices pose special problems for females. Careers for young women today are far more numerous than they were for their mothers, and parents react to this change in one of at least three ways.

First, some parents feel that a woman's "only place" is in the home, that she should limit her interests and goals to becoming a wife and a mother. Some parents deny their daughters **39** the chance for a college education by using the argument "It isn't necessary to spend all that money to be a housewife." The number of these parents is rapidly decreasing largely because, in many families, both parents already work outside the home in order to meet the expenses of life in our time.

A second group of parents may accept the change, but simply assume that their daughters ought to be looking at traditional female careers: teacher, nurse, sales clerk, stewardess, or secretary. Such parents are likely to underestimate the possibility of their daughter becoming a doctor, corporate executive, plumber, or pilot—and react negatively to such a desire on her part.

The third group of parents, at the other end of the scale, not only makes daughters aware of the new opportunities available, but even pushes their daughters toward these careers— whether or not the daughters have the interest or ability. Their daughters become, in effect, a flag to wave at the world to demonstrate how "modern" the parents are. Such a tactic is no better than those used by the first two groups of parents.

To some degree, males also feel the sting of stereotyping. Young men who express the desire to be elementary teachers, flower arrangers, interior decorators, nurses, or dancers likely encounter the same resistance as they stray from the paths their parents traveled when they made their career decisions.

Obviously, not all parents fall into one of the above categories; some are totally open to and supportive of their children's career goals. But feelings on both sides are so strong and conflict arises so often that we cannot overstate the importance of communication in discussing career plans.

Responding to Parental Pressures

You need to be willing to talk, without defensiveness, about your selection of (or current disinterest in) career choices, the fears you feel, the talents and interests you have, the options available, and the question of higher education and its financing. If you haven't made a career choice yet, your parents probably won't be too concerned—if you show by your interest that you are considering several options and would welcome their advice, help, and support in making your decision. But they need to understand that it is your decision.

If you have made a choice, communicate your interests very clearly, along with the facts about what is involved and why you made this choice—especially if your feelings run counter to what your parents expect or believe you "ought" to pursue as a young man or woman. Talk to people in the professions you envision for yourself; write to colleges or companies for program information. Talk to your school guidance counselor or a pastor. If you can show your parents some facts or evidence of mature thinking, you will more likely convince them that you are beyond the childish I'm-going-to-be-a-fireman stage that changes from week to week. You need to clearly make known your wishes and needs, not to oppose their dreams but to make your own come true.

Christian Career Planning

Choosing a career invites serious examination of abilities and interests. Also, young Christians open their hearts to God's plan. While they want an interesting, fulfilling, and personally rewarding career, they also feel a responsibility to serve God in the best way they can. They accept their talents as gifts from God and seek to use them to God's glory in their career.

"Christian career planning" does not automatically mean church employment/ministry. Laypeople will always be the backbone of the Christian congregation. God uses people in all professions to extend His kingdom. God values, honors, and praises all honest work. That assurance from God provides a solid base for your career decision—and for discussions with your parents about it.

Many Christian parents hope their children will become pastors, teachers in Christian schools, or directors of Christian education in a congregation. Such careers are not for everyone; but when your talents suggest you could handle the training for and stress of such professions, conversations with your parents, with church leaders, and with God through prayer will help you consider these special careers. God blesses all work done to His glory, but He continues to need capable people to fill the pulpits, classrooms, and youth leadership positions in His churches. **41**

The Matter
of Teenage Employment

Closely connected to your long-range decisions are the short-term ones. Once a person reaches 16—or younger for certain kinds of labor—parents usually expect their teenagers to get part-time or summer jobs. These often begin with baby-sitting, lawn mowing, or farm work, and move on toward work in discount stores, service stations, supermarkets, or fast food establishments. While such jobs usually do not lead to career employment, parents are concerned if their teenager doesn't want any job. True, many of these jobs are temporary, poorly paid, and barely worth the effort—except for the valuable experience found in joining others in the world of work. Parents know this and are eager for their children to perform faithfully these small tasks that are good training for bigger ones later on. Plus, most parents want their teens to have the pleasure of controlling money they can call their own, the discipline of saving for a large, pleasurable purchase, and the satisfaction of tithing.

In spite of the money, though, not many teenagers really like their part-time jobs—and most see them as teaching what they *don't* want to spend all their lives doing. However, without some work experience as a teen, you'll find future career decisions difficult.

Whatever way your parents fit into this situation, they can be helpful to you—in making job-related contacts, discussing problems you're having with supervisors or fellow employees, helping you budget the money you earn, and explaining about taxes, withholding, insurance, etc. Even though your employment as a teen may not seem like much, it does provide a common ground for discussion that will help build a mutual respect between you and your parents. And these discussions now lay the stepping stones to future healthy conversations about your career choices.

"LEARN TO SAVE; I CAN'T SUPPORT YOU FOREVER"

Money! You're probably interested in more of it than you have, and you're probably frustrated by not having as much as you'd like and by not knowing how to get more. Too often, only an empty echo from your purse or pocket answers the call of a new computer game, a new tape, new clothes, etc. And your money problems may wind up in an argument with your parents. You already know the accusations.

"What do you mean, you've spent all your allowance? Do you think money grows on trees? If you'd do a little more around here to help out, maybe I'd consider raising your allowance. When I was your age, I knew the value of a dollar."

Chances are, you've heard them all—or slight variations of them—and chances are, you're tired of these responses to what seem to you to be perfectly good reasons for asking for financial help.

Before discussing the parental view of money, let's trace for a moment your own interest in it. Perhaps your first memory of money is the coin that magically produced a colored gum ball from a machine in some store while you shopped with a parent.

43

Perhaps it was the dollar that Grandpa gave you when he visited your home, or the five-dollar bill that Aunt Elizabeth included with your third birthday card. Before many more birthdays passed, you probably lost all interest in the cards and looked only to see if any money was enclosed. Later on came allowances—small at first, but gradually increasing as you grew. Then came the first payment for little jobs you did—picking up the toys in your room, taking out the trash, doing the dishes, mowing the lawn, and so on. Finally, part-time and summer jobs provided the money that was becoming more and more important in your life.

I'm sure you've discovered by now that however much money you have, it seldom seems enough. As someone once said, "I always have too much month left at the end of the money." "The faster I go, the behinder I get." As income—whether wages or allowance—increases, so do the expenses. We all have an uncanny knack of living just beyond our means, of spending more than we make. This universal principle touches all people—not just teenagers. And herein lies the root of the conflicts you might be having with your parents about money.

Parents Have Money Problems, Too

Parents have the same attraction to money that you do—and the same dilemma of having too little to do too many things. No matter how well parents budget their income, the stack of bills to be paid often exceeds the stack of dollar bills available. Car or house repairs, emergency medical expenses, rising utility costs, taxes, insurance, food for a growing family, education costs, and the desire to do all they can for church and charity generally leave parents in a less-than-receptive mood when you request "a little extra" for something you want or need. Your dad's frustrated response "Do you think I'm made of money?" seems directed at you. Actually, it's probably directed at himself. Chances are he'd like to help. But when he hears his budget scream for lack of money, your request hits like the last straw, and—probably unfairly—you receive the brunt of the attack. You he can yell at; you don't carry the same clout as the IRS, the phone company, and the loan office.

44

In their frustration, many parents look for a "logical" reason not to give you extra money from their limited supply. They find it in the accepted equation that work equals payment. Since going to school doesn't seem like work, parents rationalize that you shouldn't be paid for just going to school. Of course, school is work and takes considerable time and energy. But parents often forget that—especially when they see you without anything to do, or with time to go to the beach or a movie and spend money. If you don't have an after-school or weekend job, your parents may conclude that since you aren't "bringing in money," you aren't working. This perception tends to make them less than sympathetic about your financial woes.

But the biggest source of conflict probably arises from the *amount* of money that you spend—which probably seems large in the minds of parents who grew up when movies were a dollar, gas fifty cents a gallon or less, jogging shoes ("sneakers" or "tennis shoes") under $5.00 a pair, haircuts $1.50, and a hamburger, fries, and drink less than a dollar at the place with the golden arches. Parents who lasted a whole month on what you spend on one date find it inconceivable that you need more than your allowance or your salary from an after-school or weekend job. They may go so far as to accuse you of "foolish spending" or irresponsible budgeting, of wanting something for nothing, of buying brand-name jeans just because everyone wears them, of avoiding a discount store because "you think you're too good to be seen there," or of interest in your parents only because of their pocketbook. I hope I'm exaggerating and that these extremes appear only on rare occasions. But I fear that some of what I've said has happened to you.

Please don't conclude that your parents will never understand, that it's hopeless to even consider coming to them with a money problem. While money problems concern most parents and while some of them may be accused of laying heavy guilt on their teens, I believe most parents desire—as much as their teens do—to find a way to work together on money problems. While your parents may at times resent your freedom from the financial worries that they have, they're far more frustrated with making ends meet than with you. And it's that parental desire to make ends meet that holds the key to improvement in your financial relationships—if you are willing to open communication with them. Once parents know you need them for advice and guidance and not just a handout, they generally cooperate far more willingly.

Talking About Money Problems

The key to communication comes when you acknowledge that your parents indeed have financial concerns, when you express the willingness to help out where you can, and when you ask to learn more about money management in general and your family's in particular.

Although most of you probably aren't very interested in seeing the family budget, you should show interest in it if you really want to build understanding. A thousand dollars a month may seem like a lot of money to most of you, but you would be amazed how quickly even three or five times that much disappears in a family buying a house, operating two or three cars, paying for education, and supplying all the needs of a growing family. Teenagers often forget about such things as taxes, insurance, and medical and/or car emergencies. In order to appreciate the problems even middle-income families go through to make ends meet, you need to see the figures—how much comes in and how much goes out. Your genuine interest in money management can open communication about money and teach you something about budgeting that will help you in the future. Most parents are willing to show you their budget, though they won't want you to share it with others. But before you take a look at your own family's budget, you might find it helpful to look at a sample one here. The figures below are only rough estimates, since where you live and a lot of other things cause them to vary from family to family. Still, the figures show some of the financial realities parents worry about month to month.

This sample family of four earns $30,000 a year, lives in a house that cost $75,000, and owns two cars, one fairly new and one older. The parents are about 30 years old, and the two children are both in elementary school.

Church and charity	$ 1,500
Taxes (federal, state, local)	7,500
House payments (including taxes and insurance)	7,200
Utilities	1,800
Food	3,000
Clothing	1,200
Life insurance	1,200
Car payments	2,400
Car insurance	1,000
Gasoline and other car expenses	600
Medical expenses	600
Entertainment	600
Savings	1,200
Total	$29,800

As you can see, the $30,000 disappears quickly—and this budget has almost no allowance for a furnace blowing out, a stove dying, a transmission falling out, and no consideration for desirables such as parochial school tuition or family vacations. Savings are minimal, no "miscellaneous" amount appears, and church contributions are only half the recommended ten percent. Since many families fall far below this income figure—especially during child-bearing years when many mothers stay home with their children—you can understand why parents strain over money matters. Someone has said that the issue of money causes more family quarrels, more domestic violence, and more divorces than all the other problems of life combined.

Money and Love

Money and love shouldn't be tied to each other, but, in a roundabout way, they are. Your parents promised at their marriage to love and care for each other. They made the commitment out of love. At one time in history, providing for each other (and for any children to come) might have meant hunting down an elusive rabbit to eat in a hut made by their own hands. In our society, however, it means earning money to purchase the meat and pizza to eat in a purchased house built by others. How well parents provide becomes a measure of how well they carry out their loving commitment. Unfortunately, that ties money to love. **47**

When a family runs smoothly, the money-love tie doesn't present much of a problem. Consider, for example, the question of allowances. Most parents and children do not consider an allowance to be a "salary" or "payment for services rendered." Rather, the allowance acknowledges the parents and children together are doing their part to help the family function well. However, sometimes allowances do become payments based on a "contract"—and contracts call for specific minimum acts rather than whatever love can offer. "If you give me an allowance, I'll do my jobs," or "Since you forgot three times to take out the trash, you get $1.00 less this week."

Parents and children can't live happily when they base everything on a contractual arrangement any more than husbands and wives can. Families, rather, need to see themselves as living in a "covenant relationship" with each other, the same kind of covenant that God has with His children. He doesn't say, "If you are obedient, I'll love you and forgive your sins." He says, "I love you and forgive you; love Me and love and forgive others the same way."

A family covenant starts with love, not who does what first. Under God, husbands and wives covenant their love for each other, and then for any children coming out of that love. So parents love their children and give them all they can—including allowances—out of love. Parents not only give love to their children, parents also teach love to their children by living it. As a result, children love their parents and give them all they can—including doing jobs—out of love.

Love, then, needs to be the operating principle in the family. And once parents and children start showing love, both will find it easier to respond with more love. If your parents have forgotten this and have made a contract out of family life, you may be the one who has to remind them of love's covenant. How? By showing more love—doing more than expected—for your parents. A big challenge? You bet it is. But it's awfully hard for anyone to resist real love; showing love in return is the only logical response. You might not get a larger allowance; but if that's the reason you showed the love, it wasn't real love anyway. Other things may happen. Your parents may show additional care for you and more interest in what you're doing. Perhaps your home may become a more pleasant place in which to live. And maybe these benefits are more valuable than money.

A covenant of love in the family does not eliminate the opportunity for specific contracts. For example, the teenager who says, "If I can use the car this afternoon, I'll fill the tank," has learned an important lesson about the way the world works—without endangering the family's covenantal base. And in such a family, the father frequently will respond, "I'll pay for the gas; I needed it anyway"—simply out of love, to avoid teaching that one can't have a privilege without paying for it.

Talking About Money—Continued

I mentioned earlier that you could start a conversation about money by asking for help in understanding the family budget. As another approach, ask for help with some of the money decisions you have. Perhaps you've saved up enough to buy a stereo or a personal computer. Your parents may not know much about these things, but they like to be part of the decision. Use them to bounce off the results of your research; they can help you weigh the pros and cons of one stereo system or computer compared to the strengths and weaknesses of another. They can help you examine realistically the importance of color or style as opposed to function and/or repair costs. And if financing such an item is a problem, they may be willing to countersign a loan or credit application—or to lend you the money themselves at a lower interest rate.

Such conversations are love in action. Through them, you and your parents will get to know each other a bit better, and you will learn something about money management. Your parents may also learn about your shrewd ability to judge the quality of an item. Of course, it is possible that parents will advise against such a purchase. If their reasons make sense, you will have to determine carefully whether your eyes and heart are overwhelming your mind. And if you decide to buy something against their advice and it turns out to be a bad investment, that's part of growing up. I hope your parents won't say "I told you so" at such times; all of us have had to bear the consequences of bad decisions. But sometimes, decisions made against the advice of

49

others turn out to be very wise ones. Either way, asking for your parents' advice continues to build their confidence in you.

Christian Use of Money

People often misquote the Bible and call money "the root of all evil." That's not what Scripture says. The correct quotation is "The *love* of money is a root of all kinds of evil" (1 Tim. 6:10). Money itself is not evil. It is a gift of God, and it can do a great deal of good—for God, for families, for those who have little, and for one's own personal pleasure. God doesn't deny us pleasure in this life, but He does expect us to use His gifts wisely and in ways that please Him. As Christians budget the money they have, they remember God's admonition to return the "firstfruits" to Him. Whatever the amount, it comes first, from the heart, and in gratitude for all God's blessings, including family and employment. As money gets tight, some people cut out or reduce their church contributions because no penalties are felt—as would be if they stopped paying phone bills or bank loans. But Christians know there is a penalty—they lose the pleasure that comes from returning their firstfruits to the Giver of all gifts, and the blessings that God promises a cheerful giver. Even in the hardest times, Christians know—as did the poor widow who gave her last coins (Mark 12:41–44)—that God will never stop providing for us.

When concern about money dominates our lives, it can lead to evil consequences such as division within the family. But if you are willing to understand your parents' concern about money, and if you are willing to let your parents teach you how to manage it, money is indeed one of God's special gifts. While money can't buy happiness, wise use of it can bring happiness to many. That should be the goal toward which you and your parents work together.

TIC
TIC
TIC
TIC
TIC
TIC

7

"WHAT YOU'RE DOING CAN HURT US BOTH"

The following conversation (or something close to it) takes place in at least a million homes each weekend:

Mother: "Are you going out again tonight?"

Son: "Yeah."

Mother: "Where?"

Son: "I don't know; we'll wind up somewhere."

Mother: "What are you going to do?"

Son: "I don't know; we'll think of something."

Mother: "Who will you be with?"

Son: "I don't know; whoever's there, I guess."

Mother: "Will you be home by midnight?"

Son: "I don't know."

Mother: "You'd better be."

Son: "Yeah."

The activities their teenagers take part in—where they're going, whom they'll be with, what they're going to do, and when they'll be home—greatly concern most parents. They hear about teenage drinking and drugs, pregnancies, wild parties, even wilder car rides, "satanic" music and adventure games, X-rated movies, teenage prostitution, and gang activities. Although they trust you to know what's right and wrong, they see you as young, innocent, and very vulnerable to ever-present temptation.

51

Following the third degree and an endless list of what to do or not do and when to be done with it, parents grudgingly release their children to a way of life many fear and most don't understand. Most teenagers appreciate some parental concern, but they usually resent and resist questions that seem to pry into every what, where, with whom, and when. To teens, their activities are private, their own business—an important step toward establishing a separate identity. Parental involvement—even in planning an activity—is felt by teens to thwart that step. Therefore, parents usually are excluded if at all possible.

While parents may not realize it, such exclusion is nothing new. Ever since young people began gathering outside their own homes, parents have been unwelcome. Your parents excluded their parents; their parents sought to escape theirs, and so on back. And, just as surely, each set of parents has resisted this exclusion, whether they were genuinely interested in their children's social lives or only suspicious. If the conversation that began this chapter had continued when the young man returned home around midnight, the mother would question, "What did you do?" And the almost-certain reply would be "Oh, nothing much."

I don't believe anyone can change this reality. At best, this chapter will verify that parents weren't all that different in their teenage years, will explain why parents are so concerned, and will foster conversations that lead to increased understanding, trust, and mutual love and peace.

Parents Were Young Once, Too

Parents don't worry only because they think the world has recently become a very bad place to live. They also worry because they remember their own teenage years and the temptations they faced. The changing moral attitudes of the last 20 or 25 years may have made sin more available or visible, but sin was alive and well in their youth—as it was in all generations before that. Parents remember the temptations they faced, and they remember the times they succumbed. Chances are very good that your parents did things during their teenage years that they shouldn't have, led on then as you are now by the pressures of puberty, friends, and by the need to prove to self and others that they were "grown-up."

Most of your parents first encountered smoking and alcohol as teenagers. Many got caught up in the mystique of the music of their day, which surely was considered as evil by their parents as yours may be by your parents. Many rode in a car being driven recklessly. And many wondered about sex and experimented with their sexual feelings during those years. While parents understandably aren't eager to admit or talk about their teenage adventures, getting them to do so—even partially—will greatly help them survive your teenage years. More importantly, it may help them help you survive your teen years. Either way, the conversation will be a valuable interaction.

Dealing with the Problem of Drugs

Parents today particularly worry about the use of alcohol, tobacco, and other drugs. In earlier generations, young people tried their first cigarette or first drink as a "maturity rite" or "rite of passage" into adulthood. At times, even parents or other relatives initiated the activity just to see the reaction.

But the movement from your parents' generation to yours has brought new awareness and new problems. Until 1964, when the Surgeon General of the United States first verified the dangers of smoking, teenagers were told merely that smoking would "stunt their growth." People now know the strong link between smoking and lung cancer, that smoking may "stunt your life."

Likewise, in an earlier generation, a father might have chuckled at the tipsiness of his daughter or the hangover of his son. But the increase in teenage alcoholism—whether really greater at this time or just more apparent—has turned that chuckle into genuine concern about the extent of teenage drinking.

Neither of these concerns, though, matches the concern about teenage use of drugs almost unknown and virtually unavailable until the middle 1960s. People—teens included—are now using drugs in amounts undreamed of by your parents when they were young. Parents are terrified by what drugs do, and by **53** the easy access that their children have to them. Rightly or not, that terror turns into suspicion over low test scores, mood changes, and angry retreats.

Since you probably have been exposed to the temptation of drugs, you need to open communication with your parents on this subject. Assure them that you are resisting the temptation—or, if you aren't, get their informed, understanding help and support. Before they can help you to keep on resisting drugs (or overcome them), your parents need to understand the realities of drug availability in your world—and only you can teach them. If you can resist drugs, they will have the peace of mind that you are drug free, and you will get the trust you deserve. If you have a drug problem—alcohol, tobacco, or harder drugs—they can often help you get the help you need.

Recognizing Evil
in Some Entertainment

While parents are concerned about the evil that can be brought into any activity, they also are concerned about those forms of entertainment that overtly contain or are based on evil—satanic rock and simulation games, blatantly immoral lyrics in recent hits, and music stars' overtly sexual clothing.

No one can deny that the evil is there. I question, however, whether that's the full reason most parents object to that kind of entertainment. Certainly, many hit recordings are suggestive, but so were hit songs when your parents were young. Satanism does provide the background for some songs and/or recording groups. And it's true that a popular simulation game of the early 1980s based itself on the presence of evil forces in the world—and, by the nature of the game, allowed/encouraged the players to make use of evil tactics when necessary to stay in the game.

As a result, teens frequently hear and read condemnations of such entertainment. Perhaps the weakest arguments, though, are those from on-hand parents who complain that the music is too loud, doesn't make sense, and that the stars (assumed to be heroes to be copied) wear such outlandish clothing. I believe that parents object to the music and the games primarily because the entertainment is different from that of their teen years—which they professed to understand.

There's a second reason why parents sometimes make derogatory comments about the forms of entertainment which you like. Think of what happens when you're feeling down and you turn on your favorite rock station. The music makes you feel better. Video or simulation games provide a rush of excitement. During the course of a day parents have often had more stimulation than they want on the job and/or facing the pressures of maintaining the house and family budget. In the evening, they're expecting to wind down. When they complain about your entertainment, they may be reacting to a forced continuation of unwanted excitement.

When they were your age, parents were willing to be excited for longer periods of time. And, with their adrenaline flowing, they enjoyed the music and the rush of playing a different simulation game, *Monopoly*. Plus, they were listening to *their* music; they were playing *their* game—symbols of *their* emancipation from childhood just as yours is now. Each generation, each culture has its own forms of entertainment and generally rejects those of a former (or later) age.

Occasionally, you will hear adults condemn some of the current entertainment by claiming that the evil in it will influence you to practice the same evil in your life. Those words, however, are based more on parental love for you than on the facts. The limited evidence that today's lyrics cause crimes or deviant sexual behavior is no stronger than the evidence years ago that certain movies or music caused rebellion or suicide in your parents' generation. If a direct cause-and-effect relationship could be proven between lyrics and behavior, then we'd see a host of new Christians resulting from Christian rock music. But that's not happening.

What has been said above, however, does not excuse you, as a Christian, from dealing with the presence of evil in some of your entertainment. No matter how much you like the beat of an acknowledged satanic rock group, are you exercising Christian stewardship of God's gifts when you support that group by purchasing its tapes? Do you, as a Christian, want to practice, through simulation, the use of evil to survive? The same must be said to parents who study their astrology forecast in the daily newspaper. Do they want to flirt with the belief that something other than God has complete control over their lives and that they cannot, even with the power of the Holy Spirit, change "the way the zodiac made them"?

As Christians, we look to the cross and resurrection of Jesus and are assured that God has overcome the power of evil and has changed our lives, as well as our destiny. As His forgiven and empowered people, we want to learn from His Word how to show and speak that faith to the world around us. Entertainment based on evil doesn't help.

Again, open discussion between teenagers and parents is the key to understanding your parents—and to their understanding you. Such discussions may reveal that you don't pay any attention to the lyrics, and that even games based on evil provide only a fantasy of make-believe adventure. The discussion may also reveal that your parents dabble in astrology even without believing in it. I would hope, however, that the discussion would lead to an evaluation of how well the entertainment of both sides contributes to your Christian witness to those around you, how well it helps you to expand your understanding of the world, and how much it contributes to (or wears away) your Christian faith and life.

The Dangers of Driving

Your use of automobiles also causes concern for your parents. As with most of the other concerns, their fear is often based on memories of their own misuse of cars. Cars today may be more expensive and have more technological advances than ever before, but the ones your parents drove were no less able to be used carelessly. By themselves or with others, some parents have screeched away from stop lights, driven at excessive speeds, and taken chances that kept their guardian angels working overtime. They know the thrill of speed and the excitement of danger. They know from experience that a group of young people in a car can lead to showing off and accepting dares—hard-to-resist challenges for teens to prove that they are unafraid of death or the highway patrol. Parents also know the dangers of driving while drinking. So when parents see—or imagine—you doing such things, they become fearful and tend to restrict car usage and to make all kinds of rules you may consider unfair.

No amount of conversation will remove all your parents' fears. Even if they know *you* are an excellent driver, they also know the dangers that can arise when you are totally innocent. But conversation will help parents admit their concerns and why they have them, and it will help them admit their own foolish actions when they were young. It will allow you to talk about ways to resist the challenges that others offer, and it will give parents a chance to tell you to call them anytime for a ride home if you or the driver of the car you're in has been drinking. While they won't like the drinking, they'll admire the maturity you show by knowing that you shouldn't drive or ride in a car driven by someone who is drunk.

Examining the Problem of Language

I'm not talking about swearing, vulgar language, or even bad grammar. You expect parents to reprimand you for these, and you work hard to avoid such talk, especially in their presence.

No—I'm talking about language that you may not even think about but that boggles the minds of most parents: *speaking*— normal, natural, everyday talking, but in the slang of today. You use it without thinking because it is used by most of your friends. Teen slang is a type of private code for a group. The words aren't dirty or wrong, but parents aren't comfortable with them, often because they don't know exactly what you're saying. Of course, that may be one reason you use slang—that and the desire to be identified with your group. Parents tend to forget that they did the same thing when they were young. I remember pig-latin from World War II days, and certainly the slang of my teenage years was foreign to my parents. But, then, my parents played the same game. Before Christmas, they regularly spoke German around us children as they talked about buying our presents.

Language needn't be a serious problem, but it may take some conversation just to assure parents that it's like the slang of their day—which you'll find most interesting, I'm sure. One thing is certain: language/slang changes, and each previous generation resists as it does. Parents will most likely be satisfied if you remember appropriateness—a concept mentioned in the **57** chapter on appearance. If you learn how to adjust your speech to the occasion or setting, you'll get along fine. If you force your modern slang into the wrong setting, expect reaction.

Keep in mind, though, that some slang words of today were vulgar in your parents' day. Do not expect your parents to accept these simply because the words have become commonplace. Your parents still hear the original meaning of these words regardless of how ardently you explain that the words don't *literally* mean the same thing anymore. Your parents may listen to your explanation and even understand it, but most likely they will never accept such usage—especially not at a family reunion. Again, open, honest conversation helps bring understanding.

Putting Christ into Your Activities

God has spoken strongly in His Word about what we do. The Ten Commandments, for example, are filled with guidelines for Christians to follow. Elsewhere He tells us to flee the lusts of youth, to avoid the company of sinners, and to do nothing that would harm the bodies He has given us. He tells us to live— and even die—for others instead of using them for our selfish pleasures. Such advice opposes the advice given by the world: "Do your own thing," "Be number one," or "You only go around once, so grab all the gusto you can." Though Christians seek to follow Biblical directives, they sometimes find themselves in the presence of an unforeseen, unanticipated evil—and face the choice of joining or not joining in the activity. Although we may not have the courage or the opportunity to condemn the evil we see, we usually have the options of walking away and avoiding such temptations in the future. Parents, prayer, and the certainty of forgiveness help a great deal at these times, both in resisting and recovering from the evil that can be a part of almost any activity that exists. Knowing and believing this truth can help all of us live confidently and joyfully in these difficult times.

Your parents perhaps will never be completely comfortable with what you do, where and with whom you do it, and why. You, however, can ease their concerns if you'll talk with them about your activities. If you're ashamed to do that, you may need to reevaluate those activities. Or if you're unsure how to handle some activities, parents can help you (if you let them) come to God-pleasing conclusions. Remember, they've been there, too, and they somehow made it until now. With their help and with a lot of help from God and His ever-watchful angels, so can you.

"DON'T MENTION THAT WORD IN THIS HOUSE!"

The little, three-letter word that forms the subject of the chapter has created nations and destroyed them, begun and ended families, brought joy and confusion around the world. Of all the subjects that create problems between parents and their children, sex probably tops the list. You'd think your house was a library—mention the topic in a voice louder than a whisper and you're likely to be reprimanded.

In spite of all the problems it can cause, many parents and their teenagers talk least about sex. Actually, sex itself is not a controversy. Simply talking about it is. Although teenagers probably have more questions about sex than any other topic, they probably ask fewer questions about it than most other subjects—partly because of some parents' obvious discomfort when asked questions.

Isn't it ironic that the gift of God that is responsible for the existence of each of us should be the one we're most uncomfortable discussing? It's even more ironic that the subject of casual talk between friends and acquaintances absolutely tongue-ties those intimately bound together in a loving family.

The greater burden for this embarrassed silence has to be borne by parents. Children from infancy have a normal inquisitiveness about their bodies. They look, touch, point, examine, compare, and ask about their sexual organs in a totally natural way. In an effort to prevent a sin-filled future for their children, too many parents, directly or indirectly, immediately communicate to children that something is sinful about that interest. Children quickly learn the lesson being taught and soon stop asking the ever-present questions. And, too often, they attach to their ponderings a sense of guilt for even thinking about such things.

Recent disclosures show that the sexual abuse of children is a serious problem. For these children sex is a very real issue. But for most children, other aspects of growing up overshadow the issue of sex—until puberty, usually somewhere between the ages of 9 and 15. When children begin maturing sexually, their questions and concerns multiply by the moment.

Unfortunately, the problems of puberty, self-awareness, self-assurance, social confidence, and self-identity all occur at about the same time and feed on each other. Young teens are at their most shy and self-conscious stages. They feel uncomfortable about their bodies and concerned about the changes they see and feel taking place. They hesitate to ask their parents who have taught them not to talk about such things. And their parents, who realize that their children will soon be old enough to be tempted into sexual activity with others, are hesitant to say anything lest it be the wrong thing.

At a time when young people need great help in understanding and accepting the new persons they are becoming, parents too often hand a book about sex to their son or daughter with the direction "Read it and if you have any questions, see me"—all the while hoping they won't, and praying that their children somehow will make it to marriage without becoming or getting someone pregnant. Parents tend to leave the task of sharing sexual information with their children to the cold pages of a book, to the schools (which usually are more concerned about preventing teenage pregnancies than with communicating Christian values), to some other adult, or, most likely, to the hearsay and distortion of friends.

Parents Repeat
an Age-Old Problem

How could such a state of affairs have developed? How could one generation of parents after another, determined to do a better job than their parents, shrink into the same shell of reluctance and negative attitudes toward this great gift of God? Although today's secular society is fairly open about sex and more able to communicate the joy of sexuality than ever before, too many Christians still focus on the negative.

There are reasons why some parents react that way. First, such parents blame their own parents for not teaching them to be honest, open, and joyful about sex. You might react the same way when you're a parent—but I pray not.

Second, today's parents are uncomfortable because sex is so open—everywhere. Directly or by implication, society includes sex in almost every medium—television programs (especially video rock), books, ad campaigns, country music, what have you. Most of these, filled with premarital sex, promiscuity, and blatant adultery, present an image of sexuality opposed to what God intended. Christians ought to proclaim loudly and clearly—to their children, to each other, and to the world—the beauty of marital sex that God initiated and continues to bless. That ought to be what we proclaim, but most parents don't—because they greatly fear that their children will try it out before marriage. And, for whatever reason, parents view that sin as only one small step below the sin of unbelief.

See why it's such a problem? Here you sit with all the questions, and there your parents sit with the answers. Neither party talks, and both pretend there's no problem to talk about. Obviously, we need to find a way, first to make each other comfortable, and then to have honest, serious talks about all those things on our minds.

When Sex Is Mixed with Fear

If you do have conversations with your parents about sex, the talking will be tougher on them than on you. You, at least, have received the basic facts of reproduction in school or church.

When your parents were young, sexual information was communicated largely in a "thou shalt not" format. And to make sure that they didn't, their parents used fear—fear of pregnancy, fear of disease, fear of loss of reputation.

Generally, the approach worked for many young people. Some people in your parents' generation were afraid of sex, afraid of getting pregnant, afraid of catching venereal disease from public toilet seats, terrified that a premarital pregnancy would end their hopes of success and happiness and make them the scandal of society. They had all the fear they needed, but not always the solid Christian moral values on which sex ought to be based.

Parents who use the same approach today face failure. Your generation has seen most of the fears removed. Pregnancy can be avoided through a variety of readily-obtainable contraceptives or legal (but sinful) abortion. Society now more readily accepts unmarried mothers into the mainstream of life. And ordinary venereal disease can be quickly and quietly treated and cured. However, instead of trusting in the power of the Gospel as the Holy Spirit transforms lives, some parents secretly rejoice over the outbreak of herpes and AIDS, the new fears to force good behavior.

Discussing Sex Openly with Parents

Instead of focusing on fears to repress immorality, parents need to help you understand and celebrate the blessings of love in Christian marriage and the sex that grows naturally from such a love. "Perfect love drives out fear," says the Bible (1 John 4:18). That statement certainly is appropriate here. You need to find a way to get your parents to talk openly about the love they feel for each other and the natural sexual desires that reflect their love. Young people need to be able to turn to their parents to discover the answers to "everything you wanted to know about sex but were afraid to ask," and to hear from their lips about "the joy of sex."

But how do you start such a conversation? Are you afraid that, if you ask questions about intercourse or reproduction or masturbation, you will get an immediate, fear-filled lecture on the dangers and consequences? You might—for a while. But if, instead of being defensive, you listen patiently and then ask follow-up questions, if you ask about your parents' feelings and experiences, you might get them to realize that you are seriously interested—not in sinning, but in avoiding sin's power and in structuring your life for a Christian marriage, home, and family.

If you ask a few questions, you may also discover a parent who says, "Wow—and I thought you'd never ask." Your parents may be waiting for you to come to them, not wanting to embarrass you or to push you ahead with information you don't want or need. They may fear feeling like the father of a six-year-old who asked where he came from. The father set out on a full lecture about conception and reproduction, using all the proper terms. The boy finally interrupted, "But I thought I came from Philadelphia."

When you want some information, advice, or help, ask for what you need at the moment, thank your parents for the answers, and indicate you'll be back for more in the future. As a side benefit, when you can communicate with your parents about the subject of sex, other topics will seem easier; and you'll begin to feel like an adult, like your parents' friend instead of a little kid.

The Joy of Christian Sexuality

Dealing with one's own awakening sexuality is not easy, not even for Christians. No aspect of growing up has more frustrations. You feel so many new sensations that you don't know what to do. You're growing rapidly; you feel awkward; you dislike the way you look; you feel embarrassed and tongue-tied around members of the opposite sex. All these things are perfectly natural; and experienced, Christian adults can help you survive and even benefit from these years. That's where your parents come in. They're the "old pros" in your life. You may be reluctant to admit it, but they *do* know what you're going through; they've been there. They may not like to remember those difficult days, but their married life is the result of that struggle. Their Christian home gives evidence that Christian marriage is a lot more than sex. Such a marriage demonstrates love in all its aspects—commitment to each other and to the family, sharing joy and sorrow, good times and bad, forgiving each other, sharing hard work and relaxation, touching and hugging and laughing and crying, and helping children grow up into separate identities with their own careers and marriages.

Of course, not all families are like this. Nor are any like this all the time. That's why the presence of God in family life, in sexuality, is so important. God created His children as sexual beings, needing each other to love and to uplift. He ordained men and women to marry and to create new life by sharing their sexuality joyfully with each other. He taught them true love and forgiveness by loving them enough to sacrifice His own Son to forgive all the sins they have ever committed or will commit. God blesses the family that keeps Him in its midst. And, as you invite Him to join your discussions, He helps your communication about sex, this great potential for joy and pleasure and beauty.

"WHAT DO YOU MEAN, YOU DON'T LIKE CHURCH?"

"Aw, Mom, do I have to go to church today? It's always so boring!"

"But I don't want to go to youth group. All they ever do is play stupid games and pray a lot."

"Why do preachers have such long prayers? I can't stand still (kneel) that long."

"You and Mom always stand around talking for hours after church every Sunday. Why are we always the last ones to leave?"

"I hate going to church."

Do your comments about church sound anything like these? If you're a typical teenager, they might. In fact, most teens say the same things. You are not alone in your feelings about religion. Most teens run into such conflicts with parents who apparently feel comfortable with church and its associated activities. That doesn't surprise me. I need only to look at the many young adults who leave the church as soon as they aren't forced to go by their parents.

I assumed in an earlier chapter, and I'm assuming it now, that you are a Christian and that you want to find joy and pleasure in serving your Savior. If that assumption is correct, your frustrations probably lie with the practices in the church and its seeming insensitivity to the needs of teenagers—and/or with a difference of opinion about church between you and your parents. Once again, understanding will help—a lot more than dropping out.

Your Frustrations Aren't Unique

Your parents went through the same period of questioning that you are going through now. If you can get them to talk about those feelings from their youth, most of them will tell you how their parents had to force them to go to church regularly, to participate in the worship, to sit still during the sermon, and to stand still or kneel during the prayers. They too were turned off by the seeming irrelevance of the sermon and its applicability to adults only. Many parents will speak well of their youth group, but will remember the social aspects more than the religious ones.

A generation or so ago, for many the church provided the focus of social activity. For some parents, it still does. But not for teenagers today. True, more churches are making strong efforts to build active and exciting youth groups. Yet even these churches acknowledge that homework and other school activities, civic groups, friends outside the congregation, and after-school/weekend jobs almost cancel out the efforts. Some churches have given up trying to compete. Some parents, likewise, have resigned themselves to not pushing attendance at youth group and church in order to avoid the inevitable arguments.

Involving Parents in the Problem

Because you are a Christian and because of the way you were brought up, you probably would like the situation to be different. You appreciate Christ's assurance of salvation and God's strength for daily living. But the frustrations mentioned earlier are real. And it's almost impossible for young people to cause any real changes in a congregation. Only the strong voices of a considerable number of adults have much of a chance of getting that done.

Parents can help. Most of them belong to a congregation and may hold an office. That gives them the power you need to effect change. But before parents will do anything, they need to understand and appreciate your needs. Even though they had many of the same feelings and frustrations you do about church, they may have forgotten. If so, help them remember, because only when they put themselves in your place will they care enough to use their power.

So the first step is conversation, just as it has been with all the other things we've been talking about in this book. Get them to talk about their memories of church when they were young. Don't challenge them with accusations such as "I'll bet you hated church when you were young!" Rather, lead them with such questions as "Did you ever feel like church was a waste of time when you were young?" I can't guarantee it, but I suspect that you'll hear many a story about how they passed notes to a friend during the sermon, made paper airplanes out of the service folder or bulletin, watched little kids fight in the pews or chairs ahead, dreamed about Sunday afternoon plans, or slept until their parents woke them. As one technique to escape boredom, I used to read the hymnal upside down during sermons and while singing. To this day I can stand in front of my wife and read upside down the newspaper article she's reading. I also remember trying to let the hymnal flop open to the exact middle or to the next hymn—keeping count of the number of my tries. I doubt that your parents were quite so strange, but many of them will have similar stories to tell.

The point is not for you to view worship as you do acne—something to survive or outgrow. Rather, once your parents identify with your problems, your joint efforts can initiate some changes. You will need reinforcement from friends and their parents. The group needs to come with ideas to the youth board/church council and the pastor. The process takes time. You will have setbacks and disappointments but change can come. The first step, though, is communication with your own parents about your interest in church.

As one example, consider what might be done to get the sermon directed toward youth, as well as adults. First, share your hopes with your parents. Encourage them to help you approach the pastor with your concerns. Pastors usually are pleased to hear positive feedback, but you'll have to be very diplomatic about anything negative. Most pastors are very sensitive about their sermons; they have spent long hours researching and preparing this key activity of their week, and most aren't going to be too receptive. But, if you can talk to your pastor in a noncritical way, simply reminding him of the needs and interests of young people, you may make some headway. Pastors already know the difficulty of working with young people. So linking your concern with his might lead to some change. Most pastors will consider including more sermon references to young people or stories dealing with contemporary issues. Some may even be willing to limit the length. Realistically, though, if major conflict with the pastor seems inevitable, don't push. The topic is very close to most pastors' self-image.

When the Music Hurts Your Ears

If sermons aren't your greatest concern, maybe the music is—the hymns, choir selections, before- and after-service music, and the liturgy. Much of the music may seem utterly foreign to anything else you hear in your world, and you may feel that it adds little to your worship experience.

You may be surprised when you raise this subject with your parents. They too may be dissatisfied with the music—but for a different reason. Whatever else people are—Christians included—they are creatures of habit. They like the security of the known, the comfort of the expected. Thus, many adults would like to limit the hymns to their "tried and true" favorites. And if your congregation recently went to a new form of worship, they may be especially disappointed. Keep in mind, though, that while you and your parents may agree that the music isn't what you like, your solutions may be far different. But that's something to take up later.

Once again, you can team up to approach the pastor or church musician for help. They won't cut out or change all you dislike, but your concern may encourage them, for example, to teach the liturgy slowly, adapt it slightly, and explain its function in the service. Likewise, they may introduce a new hymn gently, using a soloist or choir to sing it through before having the congregation sing it. They may even be willing—occasionally—to **69** use some of the modern Gospel songs popular with youth. You don't have to recommend specifics; just expressing your concern will alert church leaders to the problem and encourage their creativity. If a change does take place—even a little one—be sure to express your appreciation to those who have made it.

Other Areas of Concern

Standing or kneeling for long sections of the service may be a problem for you. It is for others. Just look around sometime and notice the fidgeting of people of all ages. Parents and pastors usually respond to this concern by explaining that the practice shows respect for God and His Word. But you may feel that you can give more respect if you sit and pay attention than if you stand or kneel and focus only on your discomfort. Some congregations do sit during the prayers, and some never will. Alerting the pastor and the appropriate congregational board to the concern may at least get them to think about it. Regardless of how they respond, if you've enlisted your parents' help, chances are good that they will be more sympathetic to your problem.

Perhaps you're concerned about the form of the service. While familiarity brings comfort, many teenagers (and some adults) would like variety—special orders of worship or services devoted to special groups or causes. For example, sharing with your parents the desire for a youth service can result in quick action. Most pastors are willing to have a youth service a few times a year, at least. But be prepared to help out by reading one of the Bible readings, by joining a youth choir, or by taking a part in a chancel drama. That's not bad, though. Taking an active part in the service always makes it more interesting than just sitting and listening. Even for the regular services, you can volunteer to usher, help with the collection, present the readings, or play some other role.

Your parents and other adults will be pleased to learn that you're interested in and not negative about religion itself. Even the most traditional adults like to see well-dressed, polite young people showing interest in the church. Since you're willing to get involved, they'll likely make some changes. Compromise, though, should be a major part of your strategy. You won't get everything you'd like, but you may get some changes—and lay the foundation for further changes in the future. And, as an extra benefit, when your parents know that you are genuinely interested in religion, they will be less resistant if you occasionally ask to miss a service, youth meeting, or Bible class because of some other important activity.

Dealing with Other Denominations

This topic surely needs discussion with your parents. How should you respond when a friend invites you to visit/attend another church down the street that has a fantastic youth program and an "alive" worship service? If you belong to a mainline denomination, your parents may be suspicious, especially if the other church's approach dwells on emotional responses to Christ. On the other hand, if your family has long attended this latter type of church and the one down the street offers a richer form of worship and focuses more on the intellect than your own church does, again your parents may be suspicious. Obviously, they have worked through the questions of what the Bible says and which church and/or denomination best expresses what they believe the Bible says. Because they love you, they want to pass on that heritage to you—and don't want your faith threatened by teachings that they believe to be contradictory to God's Word. To you, however, an occasional visit elsewhere seems harmless enough—certainly better than a lot of other options available to teenagers.

You need to talk to your parents and pastor about this matter. Obviously, they won't want you to change churches, but your open discussion can reveal to them the full range of teenagers' needs regarding worship, Bible study, and fellowship—and what the church down the street offers that your church doesn't. Congregations need to provide a wide variety of experiences. Initiating changes in your own church will be of far more permanent value than an occasional visit down the street.

The ideal in working with your parents and your congregation is, again, compromise. Just as young people can grow to understand and accept service forms and music that are strange to their everyday world, so adults can learn to understand and **71** accept different worship experiences—perhaps even Christian rock. Adults take longer to change, but some do—and even like what they learn.

Exploring Other Religious Concerns

As you and your parents build open communication lines about religion, you will find it easier to move into the really hard questions of doctrine that you might not have understood or been interested in a year or three ago. Both you and your parents can benefit from discussions about God and the Trinity, about Jesus' death and resurrection, about faith and good works, about death, heaven, hell and angels, about sin and forgiveness, about your work to reach the unsaved, and about your interaction with other Christians. Just as with sex, your parents can help you with "everything you wanted to know about religion but were afraid to ask" because you thought you were supposed to simply believe everything without questioning. Parents, pastors, and Christian teachers may not have all the answers, but many are open to the questions. And questions on doctrine lead to other questions about how a Christian lives out that doctrine—questions on financial support for the church, on war and pacifism, on governmental politics, on abortion and the role of women in the church, on the church's role in the political situations of foreign countries, on racism, poverty, and hunger. Religion does not end with the church service. Once you get involved in its full scope, it becomes a meaningful part of your life—and most of the boredom and lack of interest quickly disappears.

You Can Serve God Now

Sometimes young people get the idea that they aren't really part of the church, that religion is for little children and for adults. Nothing could be further from the truth (although parents have sometimes done a lousy job of letting you know it). You possess tremendous energy that can be used for God's work, for service to God and all His people. You have a right—and the responsibility—to be a part of the church. Parents and church leaders need to recognize this. If they don't, you need to remind them again and again until they notice and start to listen. When you do start working together with them, the church truly becomes the force that Jesus envisioned when He said, "Go out into all the world and bring the good news of salvation to everyone and make them My followers."

MAYBE PARENTS *ARE* PEOPLE AFTER ALL

In the past nine chapters of this book I've made a lot of assumptions. I started by assuming that you are a Christian and that you and your parents love each other—even if, because of sin, you don't always show or say it. I've assumed that you and your parents have some difficulties—at least from time to time. I've assumed that sometimes you just don't understand why parents are the way they are, why they say or do what they do, and where they're coming from. I've also assumed that I know something about parents and can explain some of those whats, whys, and wheres. I've assumed that you might be willing to take the initiative and approach your parents with questions or concerns, thus opening up some communication. And, finally, I've done all this assuming because I also assume—no, firmly believe—that such conversations *will* help you understand your parents, their backgrounds, their interests, and their concern about you.

When you and your parents find out that you really aren't all that different, that back then they were a lot like you are now, I believe you actually will *like* these people whom, perhaps, you only loved before. I believe you'll find enough in common so that you'll like them enough to enjoy their presence. They might not even seem as old, odd, or out of it as before. If that happens, you'll be happier, your parents will be happier, and I'll be happier because this book did some of what it was written for.

How to Make Contact with Parents

Until now, I haven't given a lot of specifics on starting conversations with parents, techniques to make that first move. Since what you do and how you do it doesn't change from topic to topic, I'm grouping the approaches in this concluding chapter. Obviously, not all of these ideas will work for everyone. Some will work better for you than for others. The key to success, though, lies not with these ideas but with your willingness to try to communicate and with your persistence until the breakthrough comes.

Pick the Time

After you've decided to try communication with your parents, pick the right time. Life today is so pressured that teens, as well as parents, seem to live on the brink of tardiness. Deadlines of all kinds stare us all in the face. Homework to do, meetings to attend, jobs to fulfill, friends to visit, books to read, television to watch—all these pressures hinder the opportunity to talk in a relaxed, unhurried manner.

First of all, expect your initial effort to be successful and to lead into real conversation. Therefore, pick a time block when you don't have to leave for football practice or dress for a date after five minutes. Also, take the phone off the hook or indicate to any callers that you or your parents will call back later.

Then make sure that your parents have the time to talk. Turning off their television suddenly or jerking the newspaper out of their hands doesn't work too well. Rather, ask at suppertime if you can talk to them for a while that evening. Indicate that it's important, but you don't want to interrupt their evening schedule. Let them set the time so that both of you can clear **75** your minds and prepare for the moment. If they ask what the meeting is about, just say it's important and you'll explain then. (You don't want them jumping to conclusions or preparing answers to questions you haven't asked.) They'll know you're serious if you go to this much effort to find the best time to talk.

Pick the Place

Pick the right place, too—somewhere quiet, away from a turned-on TV and away from shouting brothers and sisters. Your parents' bedroom might be okay—unless that room represents a history of scolding or punishment. Your bedroom might work—if it's private and not so littered that your parents will react to the mess instead of responding to you. Or you might consider a study, den, or home office. You may prefer to take a walk or a ride, or sit in a park. You may prefer a quiet corner in a fast-food establishment (if that's possible). Sharing a soft drink or a cup of coffee can add to the occasion, especially if you do the buying. Actually, any place peaceful will work. Just try to select a place relatively free from interruption.

Get to the Point

The hardest part, of course, is starting. But since you asked for the meeting, get to the point. For example, "Dad, something's really bothering me, and I need to talk to you about it. It seems to me that you find something wrong with everything I do or say. I know I'm not perfect, but you never seem to notice when I do something well. I really feel rotten about that. Did you ever feel that way about your parents when you were young?"

An introduction like that gets your parents' attention quickly, makes them stop and think, and speaks from a level of maturity to which they need to respond seriously. (They'll also be relieved to know it's not the "serious problem" they've been imagining ever since supper.)

Your parents probably will be quick to say that they didn't mean what you thought they did and that you have overreacted or misunderstood. If they say something like that, they probably are a bit defensive. Parents can be that way, you know. Ignore it to avoid an argument. Ask instead what they did mean; or repeat your previous questions. If they respond that they did have similar moments with their parents, ask them how they worked out the problem when they were teenagers. Of course, both sides will need to learn how to listen attentively—without interrupting—while the other one is talking. You may not solve the problem in one meeting, but you will have begun to talk. When the conversation stalls for a while, thank your parents for taking the time, and indicate you'd like to talk like this again, that there are lots of things you'd like to talk about. (A long stall indicates that the participants aren't sure which way the conversation is heading. Since you don't want to risk turning it into an angry confrontation, bring it to a halt.)

No matter which subject you discuss, whether discussed in this book or another, the approach is sound. Find the time, find the place, clearly explain what you are feeling or wondering about some particular problem, and ask for their reaction to it. Once that is done, let the conversation run its course naturally. Avoid the temptation to disagree or to become defensive. Ask questions instead of making attacks. Soon your parents may realize that asking questions is more productive than passing judgment. They may seek information from you rather than criticizing.

Here's one more suggestion: start or end with "I love you"; or have a brief prayer when you are done. These things are important, but they shouldn't be unnatural or make anyone feel more uncomfortable than they already are.

The hardest part is starting. It's easy for parents and children to find excuses not to. Usually, however, the excuses cover up a basic uneasiness about discussing important family relationships. Try to defuse that uneasiness with understanding. Once you've made the plans to talk and actually carried them through the first time, it gets easier to do again—and again.

Talking Even When No Problems Exist

Problems aren't the only reason to have these talks. Some can occur with no "heavy" reason. Find the time and place and just talk.

"Mom, do you remember when you first started getting interested in boys? What did you do? Was it hard for you to talk to guys? When did you have your first date? How did you meet Dad?" And so on.

A mother approached in this manner feels younger again as she remembers her teenage years. She'll share—and together you'll laugh (or cry) as she realizes her "little girl" is growing up quickly. "Nonproblem" talks lay the foundation for problem talks on the same subject later on.

All kinds of subjects can be part of nonproblem talks, and they don't *have* to be private. The whole family can join these times. The following list of questions might give you some ideas for nonproblem talks that will help you and your parents share yourselves with one another.

You may even want to make copies of one or two questions so that each person in the family can write his or her own answers before you start discussing them.

1. What is/was your favorite food?
2. What is/was your favorite sport?
3. What kind of movies do/did you like best?
4. Who is/was your favorite movie star?
5. What kind of music is/was your favorite?
6. Who is/was your favorite musical group/singer?
7. What is/was your favorite automobile?
8. What is/was your favorite color?
9. What is/was your favorite department store?
10. Who is/was your favorite author?
11. What is/was your favorite book/story?
12. In what clothing are/were you most comfortable?
13. Who is/was your favorite president?
14. In what state would you choose to live if you could?
15. What do/did you want to be (profession)?
16. What salary is necessary for happiness?
17. What is/was your most puzzling question about religion?
18. What do/did you do when you are/were unhappy?
19. What do/did you want more than anything else?
20. Who is/was your best friend (other than God)?

Or if you want to focus specifically on your parents' youth, use some of the following questions. I'm sure they'll generate information, nostalgia, laughter—and loving understanding.

1. What did you do when you were young?
2. What games did you play?
3. What were the television/radio shows?
4. What did you do in school?
5. Did you have other boyfriends/girlfriends?
6. What summer jobs did you have?
7. Did you or your friends ever get into trouble?
8. Did you like school/teachers?
9. Tell us about family traditions/holidays.
10. What vacation trips did you take?
11. When were you most afraid?
12. Did your parents get angry at you?
13. How did they punish you?
14. How did you meet?
15. When did you get engaged?
16. What was your wedding like? Did you have a honeymoon?

Questions like these, followed up by a lot of "why" questions, will help you understand your family roots. Encourage your parents to talk—about their memories of childhood with their parents, school, buying a first car, memorable dates, childhood crushes, accidents and injuries, etc. The more you know about your parents, the more human, the more natural, the more likeable they become.

Growing from Loving to Liking

From conversation comes understanding. From understanding come appreciation and fondness. From fondness comes a deeper kind of family love than mere obligation.

As you and your parents talk about your feelings and frustrations, you will sense differences in your relationship—less tension, for example. Oh, tension will still come; but when it does, you'll know how to ease it. You'll still get angry and act immature when your parents are thoughtless, but you'll also feel more grown-up at times because your parents will treat you that way. You'll find that you really can understand and get along with these people whom God has given you to live with. And you'll notice the love you have for them as parents growing into a liking for them as friends.

I said earlier that I couldn't guarantee the success of your efforts. Anything people do is imperfect. But God guarantees success. Use His love for you and the strength that goes with it, repair the cracks that might be appearing between you and your parents, and your relationship will improve. God blesses those families that bring love out of the closet, and He helps them understand and like each other. That's a guarantee—not because I said it, but because God says it.

May God bless the adventure of your teenage years, nourish the relationship between you and your parents, and keep you in His loving arms all the days of your life, until He brings us together in eternity.